# Vanc

*Cities, Sights & Other Places You NEED To Visit*

# Table of Contents

# Chapter 1 - Overview About The Country, The People & Traditions

Stretching from the Pacific Ocean to the Atlantic as well as north to the Arctic, the nation of Canada covers the wide, top swath of the North American continent and holds the rank of 2nd largest country in the world in total area, 4th largest in terms of land area. Composed of ten provinces, three territories, six time zones, and the world's longest coastline, Canada is officially bilingual with signage everywhere being provided in both English and French. The land border with the United States is the world's longest and the bulk of the Canadian population lives in urban areas within 100 miles of the border along the route of the Trans-Canada Highway. The name Canada is thought to be attributable to a St. Lawrence Iroquoian word 'kanata' meaning village or settlement and Canada was originally home to various aboriginal groups which are today recognized as First Peoples.

Norsemen, namely Leif Erickson, briefly settled in Newfoundland around 1000 AD and further Europeans followed in 1497 beginning with the Italian John Cabot who claimed Canada's Atlantic coast for England. Further interest in Canada continued in the 16th century with Basque and Portuguese seasonal fishing and whaling encampments being operated on the Atlantic coast. In 1534, Jacques Cartier of France explored the St. Lawrence River and the French established the colony of Canada in 1537. 1583 brought Sir Humphrey Gilbert on behalf of Queen Elizabeth the 1st and he was to lay claim to St Johns in Newfoundland which would become the first North American British colony. The first permanently inhabited settlement within Canada was by the Frenchman Samuel de Champlain in 1605 at Port Royal in Nova Scotia and by the mid 17th century, the Beaver Wars (also known as the French and Iroquois wars) had ensued over the lucrative fur trade in Canada. Ultimately British settlers and the Hudson's Bay Company prevailed over the French through a series of conflicts to retain control of the area that is today Canada. Still maintaining close ties to Britain, Canada achieved its essential independence in 1931 and complete sovereignty in 1982. No longer legally obligated to Parliament overseas, Canada operates as a federal parlimentary democracy and recognizes Queen Elizabeth II as head of state.

Canada's land mass is divided into the harsh tundra environment of the Arctic north, the tradition-bound, forested, and maritime-oriented eastern Atlantic provinces (Newfoundland, Nova Scotia, Prince Edward Island, and New Brunswick) which anchor the St Lawrence River seaway and its extensive shipping industry, the Central provinces of Ontario and Quebec which form the populous business and political heart of the country while also standing as a stronghold of French heritage in Canada, the Prairie provinces of Manitoba, Saskatchewan, and Alberta- home to wheat, cattle, and great open spaces, and finally the West-British Columbia- a bastion of progressive thinking where the mountains meet the sea. 50% of Canada's land area is forested, comprising 10% of the world's remaining forests. A land of lakes, Canada contains two million freshwater lakes within its borders as well as abutting four of the five Great Lakes on the US border.

A young country, an easygoing ethos, and a multi-cultural 'mosaic' culture have left Canada with few clearly recognizable national traditions, as many citizens identify most closely with their local region while remaining proudly Canadian. Canadians are regarded as modest, practical, and logical and practice a combination of efficiently accomplishing tasks while letting all live as they wish. Often idealized as a simpler way to run a country, Canada is eyed by many (especially Americans) as a utopia to the north. Canada often is associated with several symbols, particularly the beaver and the maple leaf. The maple leaf became attached to the Canadian identity as early as the year 1700, and the aboriginal peoples quickly identified its value in making syrup from the sugary sap. There are 13 species of maple native to North America of which ten varieties are found in Canada, at least one species in every province. The beaver as a symbol dates to the fur trading era and the popularity of beaver fur hats which enticed the fur traders who heartily squabbled over the land where these valuable creatures lived. The beaver is considered to be industrious and humble in its determination to modify its environment for its survival and success, values that resonate strongly with Canadians.

Named by Queen Victoria to delineate British territory from American claims in what had been the Hudson Bay Company's Columbia Department, British Columbia is defined by its Pacific Ocean coastline and the march of the Rocky Mountains towards the sea which stripe the province with ten distinct mountain ranges. British Columbia's first residents were the Tlingit, Sekani, Haida, Chilcotin, and Shuswap tribal peoples, the Pacific Northwest being the last part of North America to be explored by Europeans. The Spaniard Juan Perez Hernandez sighted and claimed the BC coast in 1774 and was followed four years later by Captain James Cook and a succession of British fur traders. Captain Vancouver arrived in 1782 and the interior was explored a dozen years later by Alexander Mackenzie, Simon Fraser, and David Thompson. The first permanent European settlement in British Columbia was Fort Victoria in 1843 which is today's provincial capital of Victoria on Vancouver Island. Vancouver Island was initially its own colony while the mainland Colony of British Columbia was founded in 1858 by Richard Clement Moody at the time of the Fraser River Gold Rush. Moody established the first provincial capital of New Westminster and also gave Vancouver Stanley Park. In 1966, Vancouver Colony and British Columbia merged and 1781, became the 6th province of Canada.

Over 50% of the population of British Columbia resides in the greater Vancouver area and the upper 2/3 of the province is very lightly touched by human hands. 75% of British Columbia is mountainous while 60% is forested and just 5% of the province's land area is devoted to agriculture. The growing regions benefit from Canada's mildest weather and British Columbia is regarded as a leader in fruit crops such as berries and wine grapes that grown in sheltered valleys. British Columbia is Canada's 3rd largest province and comprises 10% of the nation's land area; for comparison, it's bigger than any US state other than Alaska and as large as France, Germany, and the Netherlands combined or four times as large as Great Britain. Traditionally the economy was supported by harvesting natural resources- logging and mining- but today the economy is highly centered on outdoor recreation and tourism with a high percentage of residents employed in service industries.

# Chapter 2 - General Information About the City

The glittering waterside port metropolis of the western Canadian province of British Columbia, Vancouver, is enviably positioned upon the Burrard Peninsula and is thus defined by natural boundaries of the Strait of Georgia to the west, the deep fjord of the Burrard Inlet on the north, and the delta of the Fraser River to the south. Lying directly north are the snowy Coast Mountains, a popular and easily obtainable getaway in all seasons. With an official population that just barely exceeds 600,000 people, Vancouver is the 8th largest city in Canada. The greater metropolitan area tops two million making it the 3rd most populous in the nation after Toronto and Montreal. Vancouver is the most densely populated city in Canada and also the most ethnically diverse, with 52% claiming a first language other than English and 43% identifying Asian heritage, making it the largest Asian city outside of Asia. Nearly 30% of the city claims Chinese heritage, one of the highest concentrations in North America. Known for its assertive urban planning ethos, Vancouver has since the 1950's encouraged high-rise residential towers as well as mixed-used facilities within the central city core, giving it a distinctive 'tall' profile. Vancouver has thus avoided traditional sprawl and been named one of the world's most liveable cities for more than a decade. The city boasts one of North America's largest urban parks, Stanley Park, and views are often possible south to Mt Baker in Washington State and 60 miles across the strait to Vancouver Island.

Aboriginal tribes were present in the Vancouver area from roughly 8,000 to 10,000 years ago and the city encompasses the historical territories of the Squamish, Musqueam, and

Tsiel-Waututh (Burrard) peoples of the Coast Salish tribes. Once there would have been villages in several parts of modern Vancouver, such as Stanley Park, False Creek, Kitsilano, Point Grey, and by the mouth of the Fraser River. Europeans became aware of the region after it was first explored by the Spaniard Jose Maria Narvaez who sailed along the coast around Point Grey and the Burrard Inlet in 1791. He was quickly followed by Captain George Vancouver who further explored the inner harbor in 1792, writing of 'innumerable pleasing landscapes". While the city bears his name and the Vancouver Expedition did name many natural features along portions of the Pacific Coast, the city did not exist yet and was not named for Captain Vancouver until quite a bit later. In 1808, Simon Fraser along with the North West Company were the first recorded Europeans to set foot on the site that has today become the city of Vancouver and in 1827, Hudson's Bay Company established a trading post on the Fraser River, just east of the present-day city, and furs such as beaver became a draw for incoming inhabitants. In 1858, a gold rush along the Fraser meant 25,000 new arrivals (mostly men from California) passed through the area to nearby New Westminster en route to Fraser Canyon, but most bypassed the site that would become Vancouver proper.

The first European settlement within the bounds of today's Vancouver, Gastown, was situated on clear cuts at the west edge of the Hastings Mill property. A makeshift tavern was operated beginning in 1867 on a plank between two stumps by 'Gassy' Jack Deighton, and other stores and hotels quickly followed upon the waterfront to the west. Under the colonial government, Gastown was surveyed and laid out as a town site in 1870 with the name Granville, BI (BI for Burrard Inlet) in honor of the British Secretary of State for the

Colonies, Lord Granville. It was then selected for the railhead of the Canadian Pacific Railway in 1884 at which point it was renamed Vancouver and incorporated as a city, making it one of British Columbia's youngest to be formalized. The transcontinental railroad reached the new terminus community in 1887 thus linking its large, natural seaport to markets in Asia and around the world and CPR functioned initially as the main real estate developer to shape the newly established city. Today, Port Metro Vancouver is the third largest port by tonnage in the Americas and the busiest in Canada with some of the most varied cargoes. Forestry is still strong in western Canada, but Vancouver receives enough visitors to claim tourism as its number two industry. Vancouver is also a popular filming site for major production studios and often is dubbed 'Hollywood North'. The city has also played host to two major international events, namely World's Fair in 1986 and the 2010 Winter Olympic Games.

# Chapter 3 - Getting Here & Around

Vancouver enjoys easy access by air, road, ferry, and rail. As the main gateway for the province of British Columbia, the international airport is the 2nd largest passenger gateway on the West Coast. The airport officially lies in the adjacent suburb of Burnaby to the south, a short 30 minute journey into the city center. Many incoming flights are on Star Alliance members, but Vancouver is also amply served by various Canadian, Asian, and international carriers. The award winning airport boasts many popular restaurants and shops and the cost is required to be the same as outside the airport. Travelers are advised to check very carefully with the Canadian government as to entry requirements and to have the proper documents ready when planning their travel.

A second air arrival option is Abbotsford International Airport, an hour's drive east which receives mostly domestic flights. There is no public transit connection, though it is an easily reached on the Trans-Canada highway. Additionally, Vancouver maintains floatplane facilities in downtown at Coal Harbour Airport and at the South Terminal of the International Airport. These services are operated by Harbour Air, Salt Spring Air, and West Coast Air from Victoria, Vancouver Island, the Southern Gulf Islands, and Seattle. Helijet also offers helicopter service from Victoria to the downtown heliport next to Waterfront Station.

Alternatives to flying include long distance passenger rail, ferry, or road. Amtrak's Cascades service operates daily trains from Seattle and Bellingham in Washington and Canada's own VIA Rail connects Vancouver across the nation to all points east. The premium Rocky Mountaineer train conducts tours seasonally from Banff, Calgary, Whistler, and Jasper to a terminus of Vancouver. BC Ferries connects

Vancouver by water to Victoria, Vancouver Island, the Gulf Islands, and the British Columbia coast extending north and several major cruise lines call at both Vancouver and Victoria. By road, Vancouver is easily reached from the south by US Interstate 5 which then becomes Highway 99 and from the east by Highway 1, the Trans-Canada Highway. Please note that border crossings can add a substantial amount of time to your journey for arrivals by both car and train.

If arriving at Vancouver International Airport, the convenient SkyTrain rapid transit system maintains a direct line to downtown, just 30 minutes away. At present, the fare into the city from the airport is $9; $4 is the a standard two-zone fare and $5 is a surcharge for trips that originate from the airport. Thus, any future trips on SkyTrain will not involve the $5 and the system is well used and recommended by both locals and visitors alike. A taxi into town runs $25-$30 and while car rentals are available, both traffic and parking can be challenging and a car is not recommended for those who intend to spend their time in city proper due to the prevalence of other options.

Locals (dubbed Vancouverites) divide the city into three portions: the Westside which is everything west of Ontario St, the Eastside (also called East Van- everything east of Ontario St), and the city centre being everything north of False Creek. Vancouver is well served by SkyTrain, the oldest, automated, driverless rapid transit system in the world. The network consists of the Canada Line in from the airport, the original Expo Line out of Waterfront Station, and the Millennium Line which serves points in East Van and is supplemented by comprehensive bus services as well as affordable water taxi and mini-ferries to popular sites within the city by operators such as False Creek Ferries and

Aquabus. The larger 400-passenger SeaBus connects the waterfront across the Burrard Inlet to the north shore, a journey of 12 minutes.

# Chapter 4 - Sights

Vancouver is a city begging to be explored; it's also a city that's easily laid out for exploration by foot and use of public transit. Much of what attracts visitors to Vancouver is its cosmopolitan ambiance and for some, simply strolling the streets of Gastown, the Waterfront, etc. is exactly the experience being sought. For information about specific neighborhoods in the city, you can refer to our next section down (Hotels, Restaurants, and Clubs) is which are described several popular areas in detail. If you're more of a sightseer who enjoys specified attractions, read further for a list of top suggestions for things to see and do.

**Gastown**: Gastown is a neighborhood- the city's oldest, in fact, on the site of Gassy Jack's original tavern- but it's also a popular destination for visitors and was designated as a National Historic Site in 2009. Despite recent development within the area, a Late Victorian/Edwardian look still exists throughout Gastown, as typified in buildings such as the CPR train station and the Hotel Europe. Amble along cobblestone-lined Water St, complete with vintage lampposts, to a statue of Gassy Jack Deighton himself. Along the way you'll pass souvenir shops, art galleries (including some with First Nations items), boutiques, and contemporary gift shops aplenty. Home to North America's oldest police museum, Gastown is most associated with its iconic steam clock, a site of perpetual tourist photography. Located at the corner of Cambie and Water Sts, the clock is a relative newcomer being constructed in 1977 as a cover for a steam grate in part of the city's central steam heating system. Powered by a miniature steam engine in the base and a chain lift that moves steel balls upwards until they roll back down which then drives a pendulum, the clock serves as a way to harness the steam in a unique way.

**Stanley Park:** Opened in 1888 and named for Lord Stanley, the 6th Governor General of Canada (and the donor of NHL hockey's Stanley Cup trophy), the West End's Stanley Park is one of the city's most popular spots for both locals and tourists, tallying eight million visitors per year. One of the first areas of the city to be explored and settled after thousands of years of use by indigenous peoples, Stanley Park has evolved through the years with many of today's structures being installed between 1911 and 1937. The park is big (1000 acres), encompassing many popular features and was in 2014 named 'Top Park in the Entire World' by Trip Advisor. Begun in 1917 and completed in 1980, perhaps the most known aspect of the park is the seawall which continues beyond the park's boundaries for a total length of nearly 20 miles making it the world's longest uninterrupted waterfront pathway. Roughly half of that distance does lie within the park creating the perfect opportunity for a waterfront walk, cycle, or jog complete with excellent views of nearby mountain peaks. A rideable miniature railway was added to the park in 1947 and the present mile and a half long railway dates to 1964; the engine is a replica of the first transcontinental passenger train which arrived to Vancouver in the 1880's. The park also contains gardens, eateries, playgrounds, sandy beaches, forested trails, tennis courts, 18 holes of pitch and putt golf, a swimming pool, the outdoor Malkin Bowl that hosts summer theatre productions, and the Brockton Oval used for events such as track and field, rugby, and cricket. At Brockton Point, several replica totem poles were installed in the 1980's and 90's and remain a popular attraction within the park. Tours of Stanley Park are available by horse-drawn carriage, sightseeing trolley, or through major motorcoach companies.

**Vancouver Aquarium:** With a prime location within Stanley Park, the renowned non-profit Vancouver Aquarium is a leader in marine research, conservation, and animal rehabilitation. Opened in 1956 and home to 166 aquatic displays with over 70,000 animals, the facility was one of the first in the world to utilize professional naturalists as on-site interpreters on a full-time basis. Both the first and now the largest public aquarium in Canada, it was the first to capture, display, and study an orca in 1964 and researchers here discovered a new shrimp species in 1997 that inhabit the Gulf Islands. The aquarium once hosted popular shows featuring performing marine mammals including dolphins and whales and in 1995, Qila was born- the first beluga whale to be conceived and born in a Canadian aquarium inspiring the children's song 'Baby Beluga'. In 1986, the aquarium committed itself to stopping the capture of cetaceans for display and performance purposes, though they continue to provide homes for animals who are not able to be returned to the wild. The Vancouver Aquarium is open 365 days a year and receives a million visitors annually. Acclaimed exhibits feature marine life from the Strait of Georgia, Canada's Arctic, and the British Columbia coast but also from farther away such as African penguins and the Amazon rainforest. The Vancouver Aquarium also initiated the Ocean Wide program which encourages sustainable seafood in restaurants and markets and to avoid fishing practices that result in overfishing and degraded habitat.

**Vancouver Lookout:** Enjoy 360 degree views over the city 365 days a year from the Vancouver Lookout at Harbour Centre, opened in a ceremony by Neil Armstrong in 1977. One of the city's tallest buildings puts you 500 feet above the streets below and on a clear day, one can sight the North Shore Mountains and Vancouver Island. Tickets are valid for same day return; a popular choice is to return for a second sunset viewing. If you'd like a meal with your view, the Top of Vancouver Revolving Restaurant rotates every 60 minutes. The Lookout is conveniently across from Waterfront Station and a few blocks from Gastown.

**Granville Island:** Technically not an island and in truth a sandspit peninsula, the 37 acres that is today Granville Island was originally a First Nations fishing area before being converted to modern industrial uses such as factories and sawmills. Reached by frequent mini-ferries from downtown Vancouver, the island which is best known for the superb Public Market full of fresh, local food and crafted goodies, lies across False Creek under the south end of the Granville St Bridge. In 1979, provincial and federal government authorities cleaned up the area and developed the 50,000 square foot Market. Today 275 businesses call the island their home including a boutique hotel, fine arts galleries, a popular water park, several performing arts theatres, and shops of all styles. The expansive market houses 50 permanent retailers and over a hundred day vendors on a rotating schedule with a food court offering hot food for immediate consumption.

**Dr. Sun Yat-Sen Classical Chinese Garden**: The centerpiece of Vancouver's historic and vibrant Chinatown, the Ming Dynasty styled Yat-Sen Garden is the first authentic full-scale classical Chinese garden to be constructed outside of China. A 15-20 minute walk from downtown, the garden was constructed in the a year, 1985-1986; over 50 craftsman from Suzhou, China worked with Canadians on the project and according to Ming construction principles no nails, screws, or glue are used. The prominent limestone rocks that accent the garden were imported from Lai Tai near Suzhou and 950 crates of traditional material accompanied those craftsman from China. Named for Dr Sun Yat-Sen, considered to be the father of modern China, the climate in Vancouver is comparable to Suzhou such that the same plant varieties were able to be used. Principles of both Taoism and Fen Shui contribute to a goal of balance and harmony that is found here, and your ticket includes a 45 minute docent guided tour. North America's second largest Chinatown also contains the Chinese Cultural Centre Museum and Archives, the Chinese Canadian Military Museum, and the Sam Kee Building which at 6 feet wide, is the world's most narrow office building. Other notable monuments are the Millennium Gate, the Han Dynasty Bell (a gift from Guangzhou, China), and the Monument of Canadian Chinese which is located very near to the Yat-Sen Garden.

**Robson St:** Extending from the BC Place Stadium to Stanley Park, Robson Street is a full sensory experience. One of the city's oldest commercial streets, Robson St is most known for the big-name and high-end shopping outlets to be found here. You'll also find quite a few smaller boutiques as well as eateries from around the world. Downtown's only mall is here- the Pacific Centre Mall at Robson and Granville Sts- as well as Canadian Crafts, an excellent source for take-home souvenirs including maple syrup, First Nation's artwork, and of course clothing, keychains, postcards, etc. With a total of over 100 shops, Robson St owes its early development to train tracks being laid along the street in 1895 and was originally a Germanic cultural centre through the mid-20th century before more recent redevelopment.

**Science World:** Officially 'Science World at Telus World of Science' but known locally as simply 'Science World', this is the prominent futuristic dome building in the city skyline.

Originally the large facility was constructed for Expo 86 in 1984-1985 after which a far reaching fundraising campaign was conducted to locate the existing 'Arts, Sciences, and Technology Centre' into the then vacant Buckminster Fulleresqe dome. In 2004, telecommunications company Telus purchased the naming rights though the new name has been slow to catch on amongst Vancouverites. Considered a leader in modern, interactive science museum experiences, Science World offers something in five galleries for every member of the family.

**Queen Elizabeth Park:** The highest point in the city and Vancouver's second most visited park offers stunning views of downtown and the North Shore Mountains as well as containing a variety of amusements and a renowned tropical conservatory. Nearly 500 feet above sea level, the park was originally a rock quarry and today contains landscaped gardens, an arboretum with 3,000 trees (the goal having been to have one of every species native to Canada), and offers recreational activities such as tennis, lawn bowling, pitch and putt, roller hockey, basketball, tai chi, and disc (frisbee) golf. Just 15 minutes by transit from downtown, the 130 acre park is known locally as Little Mountain and opened to the public in the 1960's, being named in 1940 after a visit by King George VI and Queen Elizabeth. Park development occurred starting in 1948 and the park took shape over the next 20 years. Within the park is the domed Bloedel Conservatory open daily, a temperature-controlled tropical garden that serves as home to over 500 exotic plants and 200 free-flying birds.

**Museum of Anthropology at UBC**: One of the best collections of Northwest Coast First Nations art is on display at the University of British Columbia's Museum of Anthropology, open daily and located just 20 minutes from downtown Vancouver. Founded in 1947, a donation of an extensive First Nations collection by Walter and Marianne Koerner in 1975 forms a large potion of the museum's holdings including carvings, weavings, and sculptures. On the grounds, traditional Haida and Musqueam houses can be found. The 1976 Arthur Erickson building is inspired by post and beam architecture as used by the Northwest Coast peoples and affords views over the mountains and the ocean.

**Canada Place:** Originally the home of Canadian Pacific Railway's Pier B-C until 1955, today's Canada Place was constructed as the Canada Pavilion for Expo 1986. It has since operated under the Vancouver Fraser Port Authority as a multi-purpose facility composed of a convention center, cruise ship terminal, world trade center, the Pan Pacific Hotel, and Fly Over Canada, a four story tall virtual flight ride complete with special effects including wind, mist, and scents that opened in 2009. Close to the Waterfront SkyTrain Station, the building is distinctive for its fabric covered roofs that resemble sails and served as the Main Press Centre during the 2010 Winter Olympics. The ten Heritage Horns (12 o'clock horns) play the first four notes of 'O Canada' every day at noon and can be heard within downtown.

**H.R. MacMillan Space Centre**: The legacy of lumber magnate and philanthropist H.R. MacMillan, operator of British Columbia's first privately owned lumber export company, affords the opportunity to learn about space, the night sky, and the universe. Highlights include the 360-degree domed space of the Planetarium Star Theatre, live demonstrations, and interactive exhibits. Open daily, the centre opened in 1968, Mr. MacMillian having being inspired by the novelty and promise of space exploration in the 1960's. The roof of the iconic building resembles a spaceship yet was designed in the fashion of the hats of the Haida people. The Centre shares the building with the Museum of Vancouver, the largest civic museum in Canada and the oldest in the city, having been founded in 1894.

**Vancouver Maritime Museum:** Opened in 1959 as a provincial centennial project, the Vancouver Maritime Museum is dedicated to telling the story of Canada's marine exploration both of the Pacific Ocean and the Arctic. Located within Vanier Park near Kitsilano, the centerpiece is the 'St. Roch', an exploration vessel used by the RCMP and the first to cross through the Northwest Passage in both directions. Other popular exhibits include those pertaining to pirates, shipwrecks, lighthouses, fur trading, fireboats, warships, deap-sea exploration, and steamships. Closed on Mondays, the museum also contains numerous model ships, a large collection of maritime art, a children's discovery area, and a library with items such as the Chung collection relating to Canadian Pacific Steamships and original hand drawn charts of Captain Cook. Outdoor exhibits include the 'Ben Franklin', a NASA undersea research vessel, and the boiler from the 'Beaver', the Pacific Northwest's first steamship.

**Capilano Suspension Bridge:** Located just north of the city in the adjacent suburb of North Vancouver, the 450 feet long, 230 feet high Capilano Suspension Bridge was the site of an original hemp rope and cedar plank bridge constructed in 1889 by Scottish civil engineer, park administrator, and land developer George Grant Mackay. Upon his death, the bridge was replaced by a wire cable bridge in 1903. It then changed hands more than once with various owners endeavoring to create a tourist attraction that continues today, having been full rebuilt in 1956. 1935's owner, Mac MacEachran, encouraged local native tribes to place totem poles in the park and today it forms North America's largest private collection of totem poles including some from the Salish, Tsimsian, Tlingit, and Haida peoples. In 1983, the bridge passed to the current ownership of local retailer Nancy Stibbard. Capilano is a First Nations name originally held by a Squamish Nation chief, spelled as Kia'palano, which means beautiful river. Kia'palano lived in the area in the early 1800's and the name became attached to the river and its environs. The bridge and park are open daily with scheduled shuttle service available from several downtown Vancouver pickup points. Other attractions within the bridge park include the Cliffwalk which takes a winding route on a granite precipice along the river using small bridges, stairs, and glass platforms to navigate through the temperate rainforest ecosystem. In 2004, Treetop Adventures was opened which connects seven old grown Douglas Fir trees with suspension bridges 100 feet above the ground.

**Van Dusen Botanical Garden:** Ranked on the top ten list of North America's public gardens and situated just two miles southwest from downtown, Van Dusen's 44 acres display since 1975 plants collected from around the world and Vancouver's mild climate allows most to bloom throughout the year. An Elizabethan Maze with 3,000 Pyramid cedars is only one of six in North America and 65 species of birds inhabit in the Garden at certain times. Open daily, other thematic gardens of which there are forty include a mediation garden, rose garden, stone garden, perennial garden, herb garden, Korean garden, and Canadian heritage garden. Van Dusen is a comparatively young botanical garden; from 1911-1960 it served as a golf club then slated for commercial development before being saved by neighbors.

**Vancouver Art Gallery**: Originally founded in 1931 with a smattering of British paintings and only seven local works, today the Vancouver Art Gallery proudly exhibits a strong commitment to local artists and displays a substantial collection of Emily Carr's works that the artist donated to the public in the 1960's. Boasting the title of largest public art museum in Western Canada, the permanent collection contains 10,000 artworks and is housed for the time being in the old provincial courthouse on Robson St.

**Engine 374 Pavilion:** The locomotive that in 1887 pulled the first transcontinental train into the city is today exhibited in the Engine 374 Pavilion, open daily and just ten minutes walk from downtown Vancouver. The locomotive was fully rebuilt in 1914 which allowed it to remain in active service through 1945 after which it was donated to the city for public display though first being returned to a more vintage appearance. Originally #374 sat in Kitsilano Park where it was subject to weather deterioration; in 1983, a Friends group undertook a restoration in time for Expo 86.

# Chapter 5 - Hotels, Restaurants & Clubs

There's no shortage of accommodation choices to be found in Vancouver as the greater metro area boasts more than 25,000 guest rooms, 13,000 of which are considered to be close-in central city locations. Options run the gamut from luxury to economical to boutique with pricing that may vary by season and day of the week. Because of the compactness of the city and the extensive transit system, you may wish to seek lodging outside of the central core, which may be more cost effective- as always, it's a balancing act between convenience and cost. Most first time visitors to Vancouver will find accommodations in or near downtown and it is indeed the heart of it all- attractions, dining, nightlife, and shopping- and with good transit connections throughout the city. Downtown itself can then be divided into Gastown, Yaletown, the Financial District/Waterfront, the West End, and Granville Entertainment District.

Gastown and Chinatown both offer a young professional scene in a rapidly gentrifying landscape. Gastown is the oldest part of town, full of tourist shops but also boutiques, bars, clubs, and trendy eateries. Access is easy to Granville St and Waterfront Station (SkyTrain/SeaBus hub). The heart of a much sought after gentrified residential area popular among young professionals, upscale Yaletown boasts a lively waterside restaurant scene including plentiful high end chain eateries amongst renovated warehouses. Convenient to SkyTrain and the mini-ferries to Granville Island, Yaletown affords a 'boutique' though potentially costly lodging option. The Financial District/Waterfront/Coal Harbour area is quiet and offers excellent views while still being convenient to transit and within 5-20 minutes walking distance to many attractions and other popular areas mentioned above. Restaurants here cater more to visitors and it's much more lively by day than at night.

The area around Granville St, popularly termed Granville Entertainment District, provides a lively street scene and is an excellent choice for the budget conscious visitor. Centrally located, the Granville District affords easy access to Yaletown, Gastown, the West End, and the Waterfront. Granville St is quite long, extending nearly to the airport; what you're looking for is the downtown street from Dunsmuir to Drake. The West End (incl. English Bay and Davie Village) is quieter and feels more like a neighborhood, being in fact an attractive residential area for 20- and 30-somethings near Stanley Park. Streets are tree-lined with low rise apartment complexes but also sport a wide variety of cafes and shops. Evenings bustle with eateries and bars on Robson, Davie, and Denman Sts and you're close to the beach as well as downtown.

If you're game to leave the city proper and might appreciate a quieter accommodation, the suburb of North Vancouver is easily reached by the frequent and quick service of the SeaBus passenger ferry, though you'll want to stick to Lower Lonsdale near the Quay and Shipyards (between Keith Rd and the water). This up and coming area has a large concentration of hotels, restaurants, and pubs and in the summer there are frequently festivals and events taking place. Basing in North Vancouver will put you closer to nature- hiking, biking, skiing, and the Capilano Suspension Bridge. You're also a wee bit closer to the North Shore mountains, Grouse and Cypress being quick and easy nearby destinations.

Another option for lodging in Vancouver is the Olympic Village area, which literally does feel like a village within the city. Just five blocks from the SkyTrain (and also served by the mini-ferries), the village is home to quite a few shops, restaurants, and pubs. There aren't as many hotels here but if you're one to like renting apartments through AirBnb, this could be the perfect situation in terms of cost and convenience. Granville Island is another popular lodging area with a quiet and local vibe. It's a beautiful setting under the Granville St Bridge on False Creek and regarded as ideal as a getaway location for couples and families. The heart of the island is the large public food market but there's also a well attended theatre and an ample selection of bars and restaurants.

Vancouver is well known for its eclectic, forward thinking food scene, particularly the intersection of the fresh, local bounty of the land and sea combined with the extensive Asian influences that exist in this port city. Food of any variety and price point is easily found throughout the city; two areas with heavy concentrations are Kitsilano and the West End. Robson St has many high end eateries and East Van is known for ethnic cuisine. Sustainability is a recent theme in local cuisine and Vancouver is the birthplace of the 100 Mile Diet and the Ocean Wise program, both of which encourage eating close to home and mindfully. Over the past few years, Vancouver has become home to an abundance of street food in the form of food carts and food trucks (over 100 at last count), generally found in the downtown area. The city is famous for its Chinese dim sun restaurants which are ranked some of the best in the world- three to try are Sun Sui Wah, at 3888 Main St, Floata in Chinatown on Keefer St, and the Kirin at Cambie and 12th. Other places to find authentic yet affordable Chinese food are on Victoria around

41st Ave, in the suburb of Burnaby- try Fortune House in the Metropolis Shopping Complex, and in the suburb of Richmond just east of the Richmond Centre, an area which is heavily Chinese in population.

The night scene in Vancouver is vibrant and varied and knowing what to expect in various areas will enable you to make the best choice for your tastes. Check out listings in the free 'Georgia Straight' publication (www.straight.com) or try a locally developed app, Nightbound, which delivers real-time updates from within the clubs on Granville St. Granville St is akin to the Strip in Vegas- neon lights, dancing, live music, and packed bars and clubs that stay open until late. Stretching from Nelson St to Robson St, this is the city's original entertainment district and today it caters to a young, university crowd who come here to barhop and party hearty. Granville St is home to several of the city's top ten listed nightclubs including the The Roxy and Cellar Nightclub. Weekends are busy (the street becomes pedestrian only in the summer) and there are often lines to enter the top clubs.

Yaletown also delivers a bustling and stylish night scene for more of an upscale 30-something age crowd, though a few celebrities are known to drop by on occasion as well. Yaletown Brewing is a favorite spot, the city's original brewpub. Gastown is another popular evening destination with plenty of bars to be found here of all kinds, each with their own target crowd. The West End's Davie Village is a LGBTQ hotspot where everyone is welcome in dance clubs and stylish lounges.

Outside of downtown, beachside Kitsilano offers a more laidback night scene and you're more likely to find the locals out here in neighborhood style establishments. West Fourth, Broadway, and Yew are good streets to start with in

Kitsilano. Main St/SoMa has an non-undeserved hipster reputation and is the best place to sample Vancouver's hot craft beer scene as well as live music. On the North Shore/West Vancouver, there's a nice cluster of bars around the Park Royal Mall and another along Lonsdale Ave in North Vancouver. Richmond likewise has a lively and eclectic selection of bars and clubs all its own.

# Chapter 6 - National Food / Drinks

Canada is associated an eclectic selection of foods including poutine- french fries topped with gravy and cheese curds- butter tarts, bannock (Aboriginal fry bread), beavertail- similar to an elephant ear with various sweet toppings, Kraft dinner (yes, mac and cheese in a box), ketchup flavored potato chips, Nanaimo bars- a no-bake dessert bar created on Vancouver Island, and maple syrup. Canadians tend to have regional favorites when it comes to food- poutine is found in central Canadian far more so than the west. British Columbia is known for various ways to prepare salmon (including jerky) and other fresh and local seafoods such as oysters, mussels, Dungeness crab, and spot prawns. As a Pacific port city, Vancouver blends locally sourced fresh ingredients with international influences, namely Asian, making fusion cuisine a trademark of this multicultural community.

Canada does have an official national drink, the Caesar, which is akin to a Bloody Mary but with Clamato juice instead of the standard tomato. You're more likely to find Canadians enjoying beer, and in British Columbia, there's a good chance for it to be craft brew. Beer arrived in Canada in the 17th century and several big names dominate the mega-brew market, yet starting in the 1980's, laws were changed to allow sales of craft beer and Vancouver has dominated this artisan scene which has exploded in the past ten years. British Columbia claims 20% of beer sold is craft made and at last count the province had a count of 100 individual craft breweries. Ice beer is a Canadian original as well; based on a German Eisbock, the liquid in the brewing process is taken to near the freezing point of water in order to skim off a thin layer of ice and make a more concentrated beverage. British

Columbia is additionally home to over 300 wineries and grows 75 varietals with Pinot Gris and Merlot being the most common. The province's oldest and largest grape growing region, the Okanagan Valley, is 5 hours east but the Fraser Valley is only an hour's drive from Vancouver. There's also an ice wine which is produced by leaving grapes on the vine until the temperature is well below freezing. The frozen grapes are then pressed to produce an intense dessert wine.

Another popular beverage in Vancouver is coffee with many independent shops and trendy cafes having arrived over the past three decades to lively, well-trafficked areas such as Gastown, Yaletown, Denman St, Main St, Mount Pleasant, Kitsilano, and Commercial Drive. A few 'must try' names are Rocanini, Revolver, Prado, East Van Roasters, Kafka's Coffee and Tea, Matchstick, Timbertrain, 49th Parallel, Trees, and Granville Island. For the less adventurous, Vancouver is home to more outlets of Starbucks per capita than any community outside of Seattle as well as Tim Hortons, the iconic national chain for plain jane drip coffee, donuts, and quick service breakfast food items.

# Chapter 7 - Must-Do Activities

Much of Vancouver's quintessential appeal lies in its cumulative urban ambiance and many visitors to the city simply soak it all in as they traverse the city partaking of various and sundry attractions. Any of the neighborhoods mentioned in the above section are ideal for simply wandering and enjoying the vibrant Vancouver street life-people watching is definitely easy to find, as are shopping, outdoor recreation opportunities, and good food and drink. Some visitors come to Vancouver just for the street and food scene even more than any particular attractions, while others come to enjoy activities which predictably tend towards the great outdoors. Whether you're a city type, outdoorsy, or otherwise, read onwards for a few activity suggestions to enjoy this Pacific Coast port.

**Hiking:** Boasting more than 200 city parks, Vancouver offers easy, convenient hiking access within the immediate metro area and many more options if you're willing to go a bit afield. Adjacent suburbs afford large, forested environments for your explorations with hikes available of all lengths and skill levels. Right in the heart of the city, Stanley Park has a well developed trail network as does Queen Elizabeth Park, among others. A popular paved western coastline hike that is family friendly departs from Vanier Park (where are found the H. R. MacMillan Space Centre and Museum of Vancouver), follows the water to Kitsilano, Jericho, and Locarno Beaches, ending at Spanish Banks. Here are a few favorite suggestions within easy reach of the central city:

**Lighthouse Park (West Vancouver):** A half hour's drive out of the city, West Vancouver's Lighthouse Park is home to some of the largest old growth Douglas Fir trees (200 feet tall and 500 years old) in the metro area as well as postcard worthy views. There are several trails here including a ten minute jaunt to the lighthouse and back (do note that the return has an uphill section). A popular hike is 15 minutes walk to Starboat Cove with views over English Bay, Howe Sound, and Vancouver Island though be aware the path is steep. There has been a working lighthouse in this location since the 1870's though the current structure dates to 1912.

**Lynn Canyon (North Vancouver):** A no-cost rival to Capilano since 1912, 617 acre Lynn Canyon Park contains as its centerpiece a suspension bridge designed to connect trails on both sides of the canyon. The North Shore's Baden Powell trail passes through the park and is an easy and scenic hike as is the short walk to the swimming hole and picnic area at 30-foot pool. A popular longer hike is to Twin Falls which will cross the bridge in a loop to return on the other side of the canyon.

**Quarry Rock (North Vancouver**): Departing from the north shore community of Deep Cove (accessible by bus from downtown Vancouver), the Quarry Rock Trail- also known as Grey Rock, Indian Arm Lookout, or the Deep Cove Lookout Trail)- is a 2.5 mile trek that takes you through the pristine Cascadian forest (one Douglas Fir along the way is estimated at 600 years in age) to a postcard worthy viewpoint overlooking Indian Arm, a fjord created in the latest Ice Age 15,000 years ago. The trail marks the eastern start of the North Shore's Baden Powell Trail and connects easily to Mt Seymour and its associated trail network.

Simon Fraser University, Burnaby Mountain is a popular destination for both hikers and mountain bikers. A total of 26 multi-use trails criss-cross the park and additionally connect into the Trans Canada Trail. Views are excellent overlooking the city and Burrard Inlet. The park also contains carved Ainu totem poles and a large rose garden, both courtesy of Burnaby's sister city of Kushiro, Japan.

**Burnaby and Deer Lakes (suburb of Burnaby)**: The lower mainland's largest lake and a remnant from the last Ice Age, Burnaby Lake was once used for rowing events in the 1973 Canada Summer Olympic Games though vegetation growth has curtailed large rowing events from using the lake today. A six mile long path circles the lake with views to the North Shore mountains. A half dozen flat trails are located within this easily reached regional park. Deer Lake is another easily accessed lake in Burnaby, albeit smaller. A three mile path circles the lake and delivers pleasant scenery as well as skyline views.

Pacific Spirit Regional Park: Lying immediately west of the city on unincorporated University Endowment Lands, Pacific Spirit Regional Park occupies Point Grey which separates Vancouver from the University of British Columbia. 34 miles of trails offer many options including an easy three hour loop through the park.

**Capilano Regional Park - Cleveland Dam/Salmon Hatchery (North Vancouver):** Dammed by Cleveland Dam (built 1954), the Capilano River has been a source of water for Vancouver since 1889. Currently, the dammed river supplies 40% of the Vancouver area's drinking water and serves as the focal point of this popular regional park. Several easy trails link the dam to a salmon hatchery where fish can be easily sighted using the bypass ladder in their migration journey.

**Cypress Provincial Park (West Vancouver):** Just across the Lions Gate Bridge from the central city, Cypress

Provincial Park is bounded by Howe Sound to the west and Mt Stranchan and Hollyburn Mountain to the north and east. Here are found stunning views of the city as well as Mt Baker, the Gulf Islands, and Vancouver Island across the Georgia Strait. The site of many ski and snowboard events of the Vancouver 2010 Olympic Winter Games, hikes of varying lengths are available amongst the old growth trees including a section of the Baden-Powell Trail.

**Mt Seymour Provincial Park (North Vancouver):** Affording views overlooking the city, Mt Baker, and Indian Arm, Mt Seymour includes several peaks within its boundaries as well as multiple lakes. 14 trails are maintained in order to offer hikes of all types for all visitors.

**Ride the ferries:** A necessity to cross False Creek when heading to destinations such as Granville Island, the miniature vessels that provide this quick and easy transport can be viewed as an attraction in themselves. First envisioned in 1981, two companies (False Creek Ferries and AquaBus) offer frequent and efficient services in vessels that seat 12-20 and afford a unique perspective on the city as viewed from the water. Stops include Kitsilano, the West End, Yaletown, and Science World/Olympic Village. There's also the larger (400 passenger) SeaBus that connects North Vancouver and BC Ferries with service to Vancouver Island. Neither are as adorable as the False Creek mini-ferries, but all provide an enjoyable way to get just a bit beyond the city's boundaries.

**Get wheels:** There are those will will say that Vancouver is best viewed at street level and under your own power. Walking and transit can get you everywhere in town but sometimes it's nice to try another way of experiencing the city. Renting a bike is simple and affordable with outlets in popular destinations such as Stanley Park, English Bay, and near Canada Place; maps and ride suggestions are included and both city and mountain bikes are readily available to rent. There's also the city's share system, Mobi, with numerous centrally located points to both rent and return the cycles. Online cycling guides abound with ideas of where to ride within and nearby the city. Another way to experience Vancouver on wheels and under your own power is to rollerblade (inline skate). Often sighted in Stanley Park and rentable from shops at the seawall, a three mile waterfront pathway allows easy access from English Bay to Science World.

**Take to the water:** Being a port city on the Pacific Coast, Vancouver is all about opportunities to enjoy the adjacent ocean. The easiest is a short sightseeing or meal cruise with companies such as Harbour Cruises, which operates four trips per day in the high season in the city harbor and into Indian Arm. Another cruise boat option, seasonally dependent (March through October), is whale watching. Wildlife cruises depart from downtown Vancouver as well as the fishing hamlet of Steveston, 40 minutes away in search of migratory orcas, gray whales, minke whales, humpbacks, and other marine life- porpoises, dolphins, seals, and birds. Cruises vary from 3-7 hours and traverse the Gulf Islands and San Juans in special vessels designed for marine mammal observation- supposedly the success rate for sighting a whale is 90%. For fisherman, there are opportunities for both freshwater and saltwater fishing with expert guides and gear included. Salmon charters operate year round on a half or full day basis, often departing out from Granville Island, Horseshoe Bay, or Coal Harbour. There's also fly fishing on the nearby rivers for white sturgeon and trout. Kayaking is an activity the locals will often say it's simply not summer without, though due to mild weather it's something that can be undertaken throughout the year. The city skyline rises above you out on the water and rental operations are abundant to provide everything you need. On either side of Stanley Park, both English Bay and False Creek are popular kayaking spots and 30 minutes' drive can take you to Indian Arm, Deep Cove, or Burnaby's Deer Lake. Vancouver is a great place to try out windsurfing, kiteboarding, or stand up paddleboarding with Point Grey's Jericho Beach being the city's hotspot for rentals and instruction. Advanced windsurfers and kiteboarders may appreciate Acadia Beach and Spanish Banks, which enjoy strong northwest winds.

**Shop an outdoor market:** Vancouver is home to several iconic outdoor marketplaces, Granville Island being perhaps the best known, but also popular and well visited are the Punjabi Market and Richmond's Night Market. Punjabi Market (Little India): the heart of Vancouver's Indo-Canadian population is easily accessed by transit from downtown and extends along Main St starting at East 48th Ave through 51st. Immigrants from the Punjab- an Indian state on the border with Pakistan- began to arrive in British Columbia as lumber workers over a century ago. In the 1970's a larger influx created this residential and shopping district which has become inhabited by those from a wide range of Southwest Asian countries. Shops peddle fashions and fabrics, jewelry, Indian groceries, fresh spices and produce, and of course Indian cuisine. Additionally, the Sikh temple at the foot of Ross St is open for visitors. Richmond Night Market: From May through October the suburb of Richmond hosts two award winning outdoor markets known primarily for the food but also entertainment, shopping, and a festive night scene that sees 30,000 visitors on summer evenings. The suburb population is 65% Asian so both the outdoor market and the Panda Market (previously called the International Summer Night Market) have strong Asian influences in cuisine and items for sale. Operating since the early 2000's, the two markets contain hundreds of food stalls and are open weekends from 7 pm until 10 pm. North Vancouver also has a similar Shipyards market on Friday nights at Shipbuilder's Square neat Lonsdale Quay that features natural British Columbia made products.

**Take in an organized tour:** Let someone else show you the sights of the city and beyond. Maybe you'd enjoy a narrated bus that hits all the top spots or maybe you want a smaller and more customized tour that focuses on a single theme- whatever your preferred style, the perfect tour exists for you in Vancouver. Options include culinary, beer tasting, helicopter, floatplane, hop on-hop off trolley, and much more. Architectural walking tours are conducted by the Heritage Foundation, local guides will show you their Chinatown and Gastown, and at night 'Forbidden' Vancouver's past comes alive in the city's hidden nooks and crannies.

**Relax on the city's iconic beaches:** While it may not be the first thing you associate with the city, Vancouver's beaches are much beloved by locals and an integral piece in the city's coastal vibe. Vancouver's beaches are easily accessed and enjoyed by all; favorites include:

**Jericho:** Perhaps offering the best views of the North Shore mountains and the city skyline, Jericho Beach is just far enough from downtown (20 minutes) to be a bit quieter. Located on English Bay's south shore and centered around the Jericho Sailing Centre, this long, sandy family friendly beach is ideal for sailing, strolling, kayaking, fishing, and picnicking. There's enough room here for pursuits such as volleyball and tennis and a chance to feel both away from and close to the city.

Kitsilano. Oft compared to Southern California's Venice Beach, Kitsilano (Kits to locals) is Vancouver's glamorous beach, the place to see and be seen. Along with people watching, excellent scenery is found at Kits as is the pool-nearly three times Olympic size, heated, saltwater, the longest in the country, and well divided to accommodate swimmers of all levels. Swimming is also possible in the ocean here as the waves are calm and activities such as volleyball, tennis, jogging, and basketball are easily found. Located 15 minutes from downtown, this is an urban and family friendly beach- look elsewhere for secluded and peaceful.

**Wreck Beach:** Canada's award winning first and largest clothing-optional beach, is much beloved for its relaxed and welcoming atmosphere as well as the natural beauty that is found here. Located 25 minutes from downtown adjacent to the University of British Columbia, a short hike through the forest is involved to reach the beach. On summer weekends, 14,000 people may visit the beach which is also known for its Vendors Row peddling ready made food, jewelry, sarongs, and more.

**Spanish Banks:** Named by the British to commemorate Spanish explorers of 1792, Spanish Banks is a local favorite 25 minutes from downtown. The beach stretches alongside the western coast of the city, making it seem removed from the urban core. One of the city's least crowded beaches, Spanish Banks affords an expansive view of the ocean and mountains.

English Bay. Another iconic urban beach, the West End's English Bay beach touches the edge of Stanley Park and is one if the city's best for swimmers. Walkable from most downtown hotels, English Bay provides sandy beach on one side of Denman St and trendy shops and eateries on the other, making it a perfect stop for rollerbladers and finding ice cream.

**Stanley Park's Second and Third Beaches:** Named for their sequential spots along the seawall, Second and Third Beaches are well used by picnickers and those watching the sunset. Second Beach in the park's southwest corner is sunny and busy with views of English Bay while the more secluded Third Beach is on the west side of the park. Second Beach has a large, popular heated outdoor pool.

# Chapter 8 - Other Must-Visit Nearby Places

Vancouver's appeal lies both in the city itself but also in the proximity it has to so much within close reach. Being nestled where the mountains meet the sea means there are easy opportunities within 1-2 hours of Vancouver to explore various sections of British Columbia including the iconic coastline and North Shore Mountains but also the fertile wine country of the Fraser Valley.

**Vancouver Island:** Just a quick ferry ride away from the city lies North American's largest west coast island, home to the British heritage ambiance of the provincial capital of Victoria as well as the lush forests that extend north the length of the island. Originally a timber based economy, Vancouver Island is now a haven for outdoor enthusiasts that come to enclaves such as Nanaimo and Tofino in this, the mildest climate in Canada. Victoria is an easy ferry ride from Vancouver and offers numerous use friendly attractions in the central core area such as the Royal BC Museum and Craigdarroch Castle while renowned Butchart Gardens is 14 miles north of town. A 90 minute drive will take you to Nanaimo, a hub for regional adventuring and the birthplace of the Nanaimo desert bar. The North and South Gulf Islands are also just within reach of Vancouver, being efficiently served by BC Ferries and these numerous isles in the Strait of Georgia offer a chance to escape briefly to an idyllic landscape known for its resident artists, farms, wineries, and outdoor pursuits.

**North Shore Mountains:** These rugged peaks that overlook Vancouver lie only 20 minutes away and thus serve as the city's backyard playground. The greater metro area dead ends at this range, which is composed of six mountains within two suburban communities. The range then extends north as the Coast Mountain Range as far as Alaska. 4,000 feet tall Grouse Mountain is perhaps the best known, with the legendary Grouse Grind trail being lovingly referred to as Mother Nature's Stairmaster. Composed of 2,830 steps, the Grind trail rises 2,800 feet and has an average grade of 17%. Also to be found at Grouse Mountain is an 8-minute aerial tramway ride, an observation platform suspended 20 stories up from a wind turbine ('The Eye of the Wind'), a wildlife refuge, and the 100 seat mountaintop 'Theater In The Sky'. Summer affords opportunities for activites such as ziplining, lumberjack and birds of prey shows, disc golf, paragliding, and helicopter tours while in the winter skiing, snowboarding, snowshoeing, sleigh rides, and ice skating are popular pastimes at Grouse.

Cypress and Seymour are the other members of the nearby triad of peaks, all of which deliver an abundance of possible hikes through lush and dense forests, all with stunning camera-friendly views. A little further away from the city (90 minutes) are the mountains of Whistler and Blackcomb, opened in 1966 and serving as an Alpine and Nordic event venue for the 2010 Olympic Games. Forming the largest ski area in North American with 37 lifts and over 200 marked runs, Whistler Blackcomb regularly places on Top Lists for cross-country skiing, snowshoeing, backcountry skiing, snowmobiling, and heli-skiing. Summer offers other adventures such as hiking, camping, kayaking, rafting, windsurfing, fishing, and mountain biking, as well as the ambiance of a charming, pedestrian village.

**Wine Country:** Only an hour from Vancouver lies the Fraser Valley, home to half of the province's agricultural production and a hotspot for boutique wineries; 30

vineyards and 15 wineries can be found centered around the communities of Langley and Abbotsford. White wines are well suited to the climate making Chardonnay and Germanic white varietals easy finds but also grown here are early-ripening red wines such as Pinot Noir and fruit wines. An easy day trip to the Fraser Valley can be arranged through tour operators (often in a private vehicle) or by your own auto transportation.

# Chapter 9 - Essentials - Weather, Costs, & Other 'How to' Matters

Visiting Vancouver is easily done during any season, as the city has been a popular visitor destination for years and thus has all the appropriate infrastructure as detailed above (airports, hotels, public transit). A common question, however, is always 'when is best to go' and the answer will surely depend on what is most important to you and of course the balancing art of various factors that apply at each particular time. Summer will certainly have the reliably best weather and the season of sunshine will showcase Vancouver's outdoor life with abundant festivals and events within the city. It's a great choice if you want to partake in outdoor pursuits such as hiking or water sports, yet summer will also have the most crowds and highest prices as a natural result of being the most popular time weatherwise. Winter is by contrast less crowded and more affordable but you lose out on hours of sunlight and days can be overcast and drizzly. Winter is a good choice for a slower pace and many of Vancouver's attractions are indoors thus enjoyable regardless of weather. Of course, those who come for winter sports such as skiers will find winter in Vancouver a perfect choice. For those who want to balance the two, the 'shoulder seasons' of spring and fall have mild weather that is neither too hot nor too cold and are less busy and costly than high season yet offer more outdoor opportunities than winter.

Vancouver's climate is Canada's warmest and winter in the city itself rarely sees significant snow- though the mountains nearby certainly do. Rain is abundant, however, with 160 rainy days in a typical year totaling 45 inches making Vancouver Canada's 3rd wettest city. Summers are pleasantly warm and moderated by the ocean, rarely surpassing 85 degrees. Daylight is another consideration as Vancouver is above the 49th parallel meaning summer days may have 17 hours but winter days by contrast contain only eight hours of daylight.

Visitors to Vancouver will require a current, valid passport-gone are the days when those from the United States can cross the border simply with a birth certificate and driver's license. If entering by land, expect to be asked details of your visit (purpose, duration, location of your accommodation). Vancouver's airport is a busy international gateway, so whether by land or air, allow ample time to properly enter into Canada. It's wise and highly recommended to check Canadian governmental websites as well as there may be laws that apply for specific individuals to enter and documents may need to be assembled in advance of your travels if certain situations apply. Once you've passed over the border, you'll quickly find Vancouver not remarkably different from other west coast cities and that Canada overall is a very user friendly visitor destination. Other than signage being always in both English and French and gasoline being priced in liters, it's a lot like home.

Costwise, Vancouver can feel on the spendy side but it is in line with cities of comparable size and popularity, meaning you may be paying tourist-grade prices when going to top attractions and popular parts of town. Seasonality can make a different in some costs and there are ways that visitors can manage expenses to suit their budget. Accommodations are often more affordable outside of the most trendy areas and smaller or out of the way eating establishments are likewise usually less pricey than the flashy eateries on tourist streets. While they not as prevelant as hotels, hostel rooms do exist in Vancouver as well as direct-by-owner rentals through sites such as AirBnb. Many of the listed attractions do come with a higher price tag but then others, such as parks, are perfectly free. Vancouver is doable for any budget as long as you plan ahead and make adjustments accordingly, and various online trip cost applications are available to assist in your calculations.

# Conclusion

As a destination, Vancouver truly does deliver something for everyone. User friendly and walkable, Vancouver delivers authentic neighborhoods, dynamic cuisine, locally crafted beverages (beer, wine, coffee), locally sourced shopping opportunities, quality attractions, and a multitude of opportunities to enjoy the beauty of this forward-thinking port city. It also sits surrounded by the beauty of British Columbia and makes an excellent 'base' for explorations of the west coast Cascadian region. Whether you find that you come to the city for history, the outdoor opportunities, night life, water sports, people watching, museums, you'll inevitably discover a vibrant, bustling urban center surrounded by incredible natural beauty and you'll surely leave having thoroughly enjoyed your time spent in Vancouver.

Made in the USA
Middletown, DE
10 May 2019

# VANCOUVER

## CITIES, SIGHTS & OTHER PLACES YOU NEED TO VISIT

As a destination, Vancouver truly does deliver something for everyone. User friendly and walkable, Vancouver delivers authentic neighborhoods, dynamic cuisine, locally crafted beverages (beer, wine, coffee), locally sourced shopping opportunities, quality attractions, and a multitude of opportunities to enjoy the beauty of this forward-thinking port city.

Vancouver is surrounded by the beauty of British Columbia ar makes an excellent 'base' for explorations of the west coast Cascadian region.

Whether you find that you come to the city for history, the outdoor opportunities, night life, water sports, people watchir museums, you'll inevitably discover a vibrant, bustling urbar center surrounded by incredible natural beauty and you'll sur leave having thoroughly enjoyed your time spent in Vancouve

# Portuguese Desserts